"This is dedicated to friends Josie, John, Megan and Matthew Bates. Also to all those who have helped with the writing of these books - including Sheila Wood, Jo Hawley, Jackie Matthews, Ruth Ham, Jane Zambra, Angela Wozny, Lucy McCappin...where would I be without their constant correction of my spelling and grammar! Thank you girls."

© Illustration and Design by Sarah-Leigh Wills.
www.happydesigner.co.uk

© JOSIE JUICE AND MATTHEW - 2016
ISBN: 978-0-9931014-2-7

JosieJuice
and Matthew

Written by Heather Hawley
Illustrated by Sarah-Leigh Wills

CHAPTER 1

Breakfast Time

Matthew is sitting at the breakfast table munching his way through a large bowl of cereal. His Dad had been busy the day before collecting apples from the orchard. He had put these through a special machine to get the wonderful sweet juice from them.

Now, alongside Matthew's breakfast things is a lovely big glass of that sweet apple juice - Josie Juice. Josie is full of the important vitamins and minerals Matthew needs to grow strong and healthy. He is very excited because today is his birthday and he is going to do some grass sledging with his friends. He had been up since early morning and had got dressed without Dad having to say two or three times: 'Matthew, are you dressed yet?' which was quite unusual!

He is almost toooooo excited to eat his breakfast! 'Breakfast is the most important meal of the day, Matthew,' says Dad with a serious look on his face. 'If you don't have something to eat and drink before the sledging you will soon feel weak, tired and thirsty!'

Matthew didn't want to spoil his day so he ate all his breakfast and drank the big glass of Josie Juice. 'Yum,' says Matthew, 'that juice tastes good!' He then runs off to clean his teeth, which was the last thing he had to do before it was time to go.

It wasn't long before Dad says: 'Time to get in the car Matthew, we need to pick up all your friends.' He shoots out the front door and into the car. In the next village his friends are waiting for him. They climb into the car with big grins on their faces; they were so very excited about their day out too.

CHAPTER 2

Josie starts her Adventure...

While Matthew is on his way to the sledging, Josie Juice starts her own adventure. Having sloshed into Matthew's mouth, she gushes down a pink slide, known as an oesophagus. With a

she ends up in a yellow pool in his stomach.

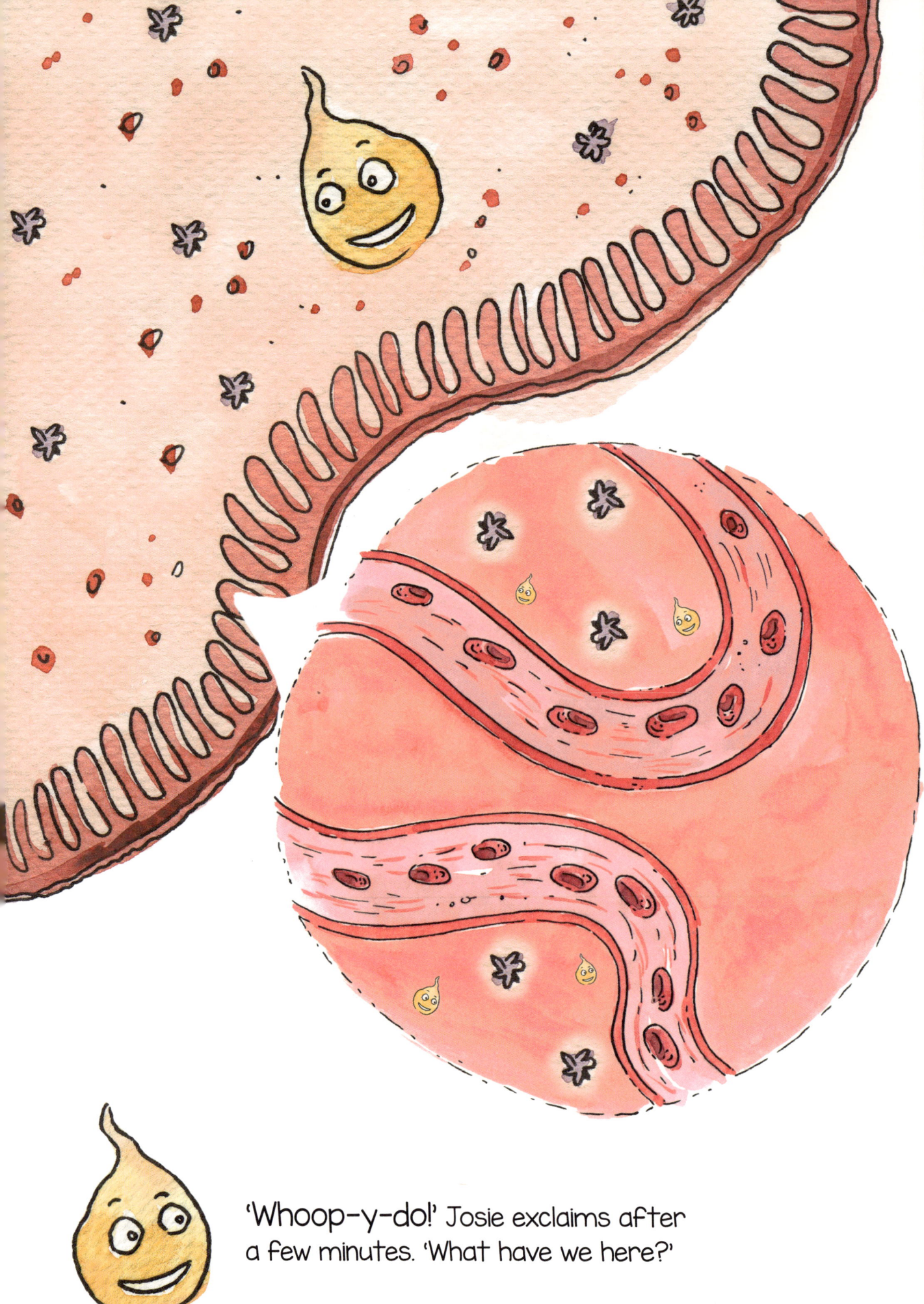

'Whoop-y-do!' Josie exclaims after a few minutes. 'What have we here?'

She finds herself in a tube called the SMALL intestine. This very
l -o- n- g tube curls, loops and bends inside Matthew's little
tummy. It is about 5 metres long, which is almost as tall as
a giraffe!

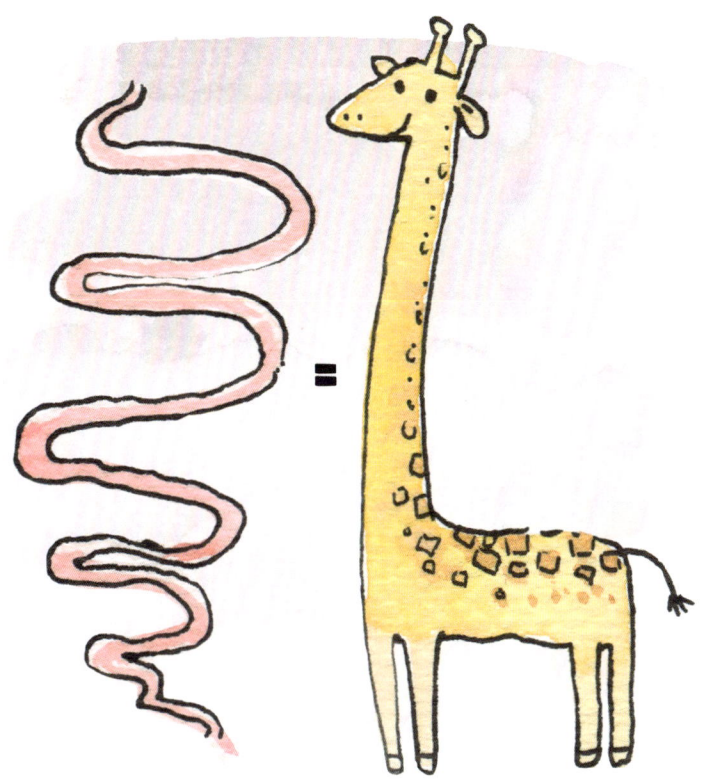

Josie finds some red liquid rushing along in the layers of this
tube. 'Who are you?' she asks.

'I am blood – Brucey Blood,' he says. 'I travel around the inside
of Matthew's body night and day through these thin, elastic
tubes called blood vessels. I carry important things from one
part of his body to another.' He seems really friendly:
'Please can I have some of your watery bits to take to other
parts of Matthew's body?'

'But I like it here,' replies Josie. 'Why should I let YOU take bits
of ME?'

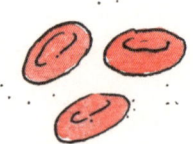

Brucey explains that over half of Matthew's body is water. The lungs he uses to breathe in and out are nearly all made of water, so too is his brain.

'Even I am nearly all water, Josie! There is water in the air Matthew breathes out, plus he also loses water through his skin by getting sweaty when running around. If Matthew becomes really sad and cries he even loses water through his eyes as tears. And because you are mainly water Josie, you can be used all over Matthew's body to keep him healthy.'

Oh how important this makes Josie feel. She thinks it might be quite exciting to take a trip through Matthew's body, especially his brain. So Josie agrees. She slips through the wall of the small intestine and whizzes off with Brucey.

Things move very quickly with Brucey Blood and it isn't long before Josie finds herself in a part of Matthew called the renal artery.

'What is this funny tube for Brucey?' says Josie.

'This,' says Brucey, feeling very clever, 'takes us to the kidneys.'

'The WHAT?' asks Josie.

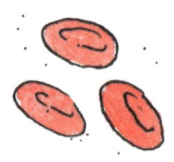

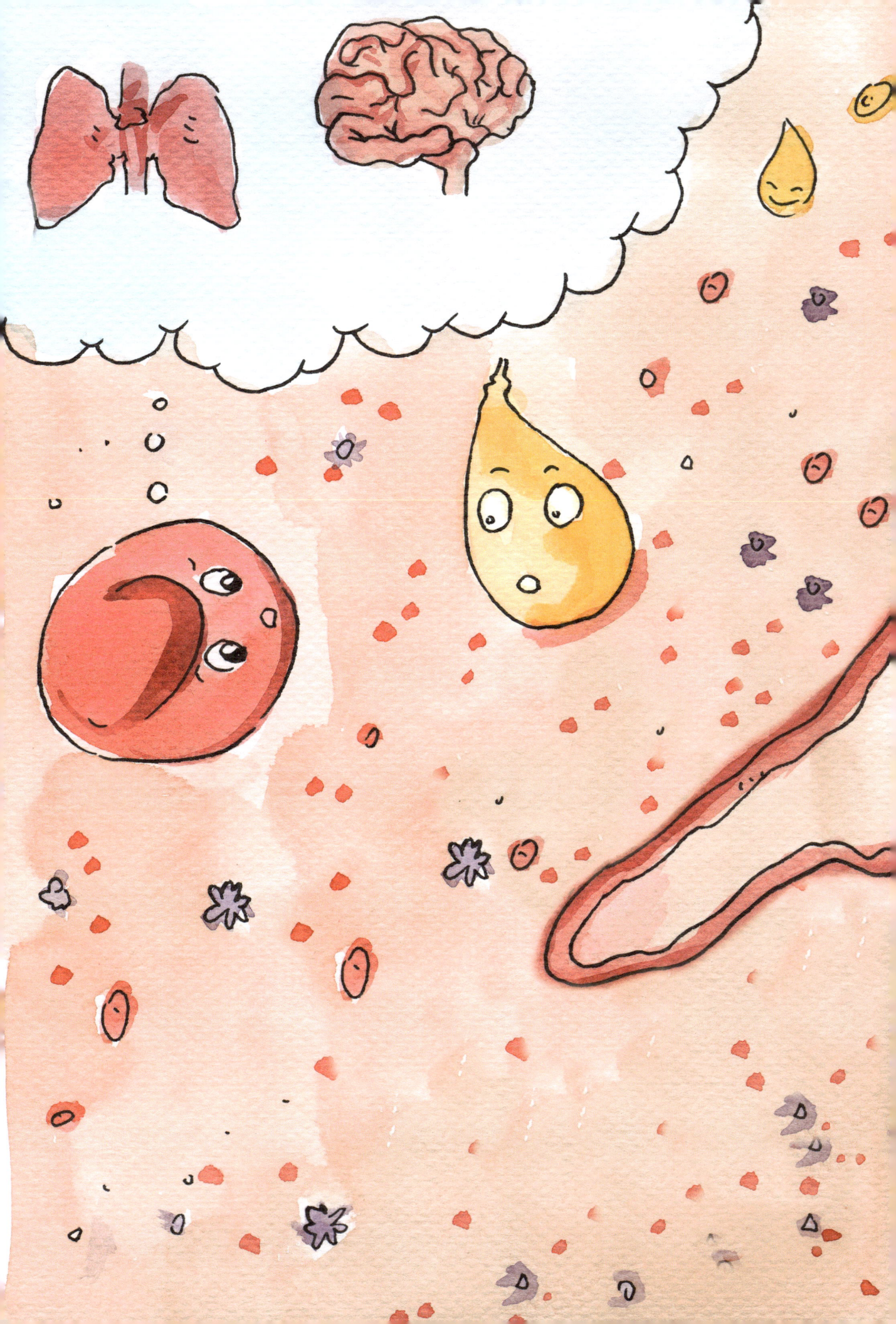

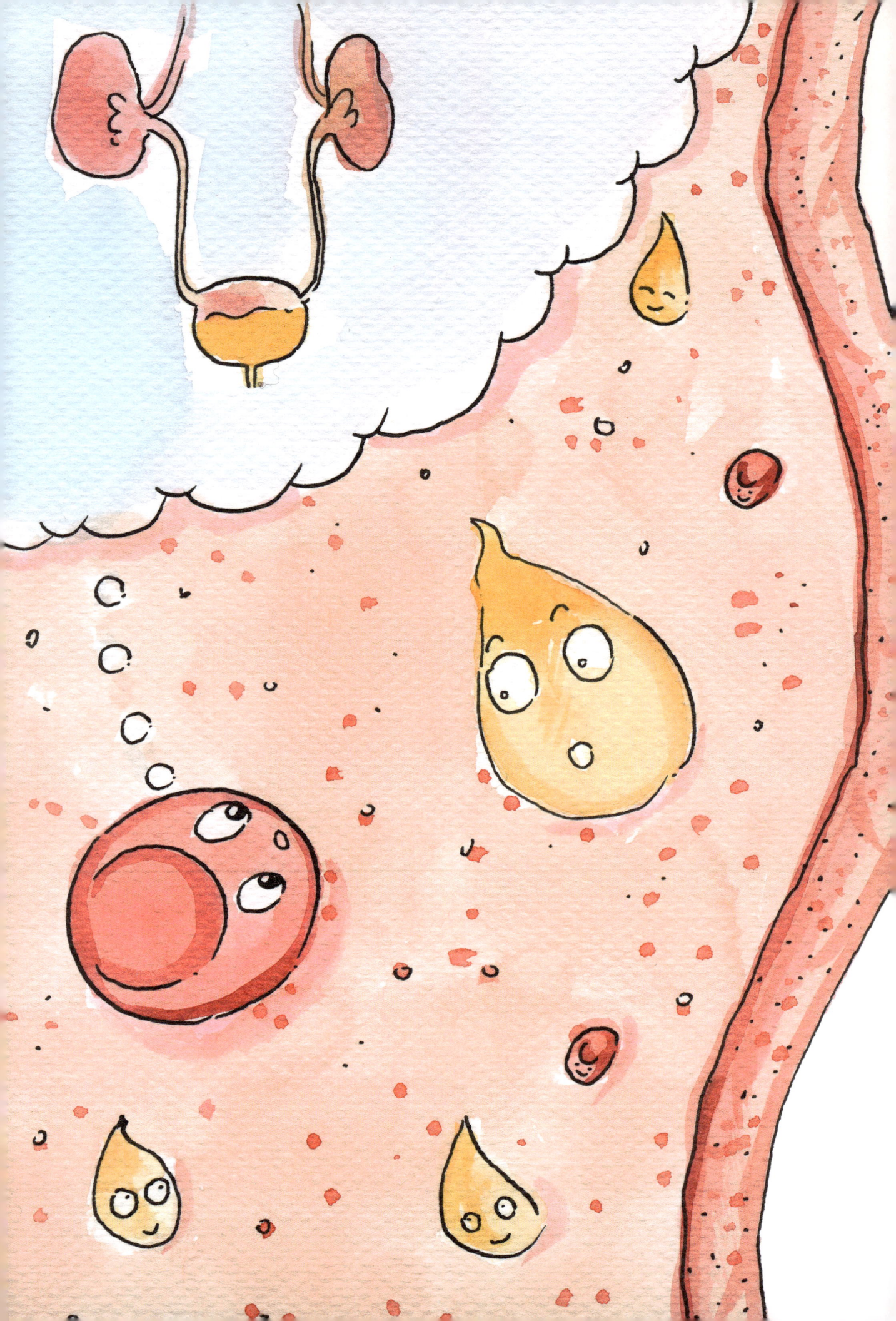

Brucey beams. He likes to think he is intelligent. 'They are a very important part of Matthew's body. He has two and they are just inside his lower back ribs. They aren't very big. They are about the size of a computer mouse. They work hard all day and night. Even though he has two kidneys, a body can manage all this work with just one of them.'

Brucey is full of knowledge; he wants Josie to think he knows everything.

'One job the kidneys have to do is getting rid of some of the rubbish I bring along.' Brucey describes the recycling processes that are carried out in your body. This is required as your body produces lots of things that it doesn't really need. Some of these things can be recycled but some can be poisonous if they build up into big amounts and might make you feel ill. Like your recycling cartons at home different parts of your body recycle or remove different bits of rubbish. Your kidneys recycle water and remove poisons. The recycled water is the pee you pass when you use the toilet.

Brucey continues: 'To do this job the kidney might put me through some special tubes up to 400 times a day!'

'Phew', thought Josie, 'that seems an awful lot of work!'

The tubes Brucey is talking about are called nephrons and are so tiny you can only see them through a microscope. If you wanted to add up how many of these tiny tubes are in the kidneys, you would have to count to a really BIG number as there are more than 1 million! There are 5 litres of blood in a grown-up, which is as much as 5 large cartons of fruit juice. A child like Matthew would not have quite as much but that's still a lot of blood to keep clean!

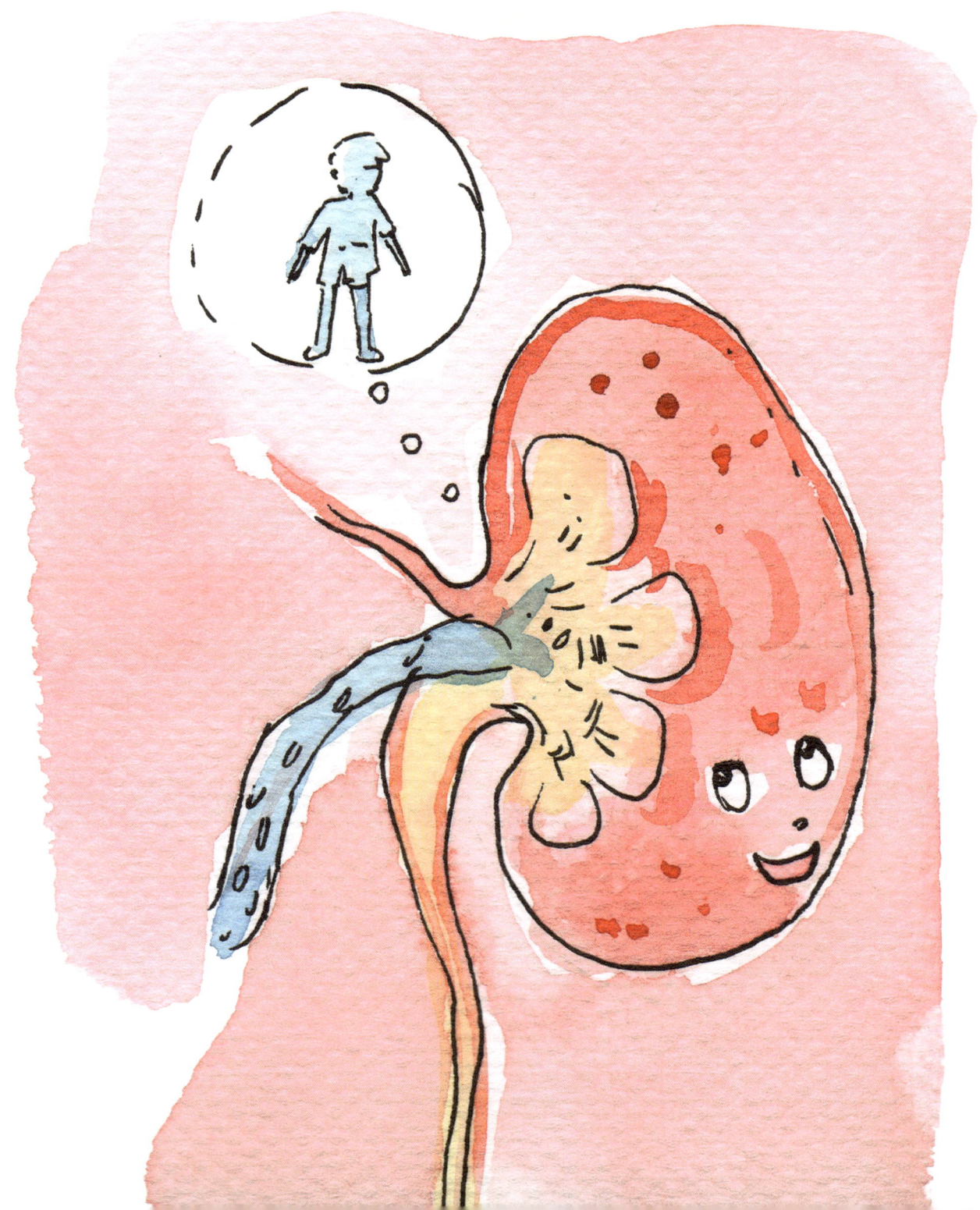

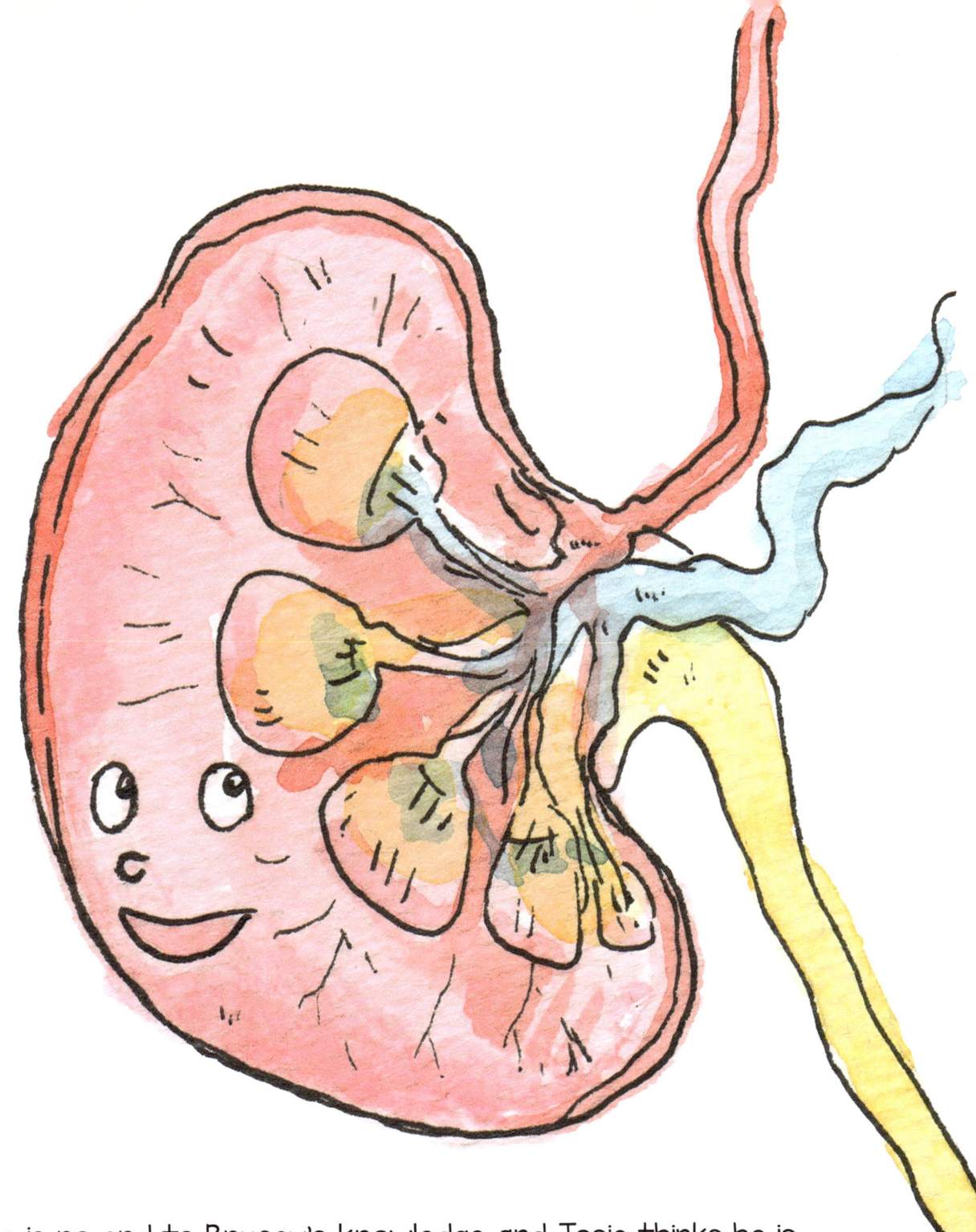

There is no end to Brucey's knowledge and Josie thinks he is never going to stop. 'The kidneys also decide how much water to keep inside Matthew, so that there is enough for all the different parts of his body,' continues Brucey. 'What's more they also work out whether some of the water can be thrown away.' Josie is alarmed, 'thrown away?' 'You had better explain to me where I am going to next!' She is worried, as she doesn't want to be thrown away!

She realises that during her ride with Brucey Blood she has lost most of her apple bits.

'Wow! Where have they gone?' she wonders.

Now she is nearly all water and Brucey wants to give the kidneys most of that! She is about to say: 'I want to be left alone now thank you very much,' when suddenly

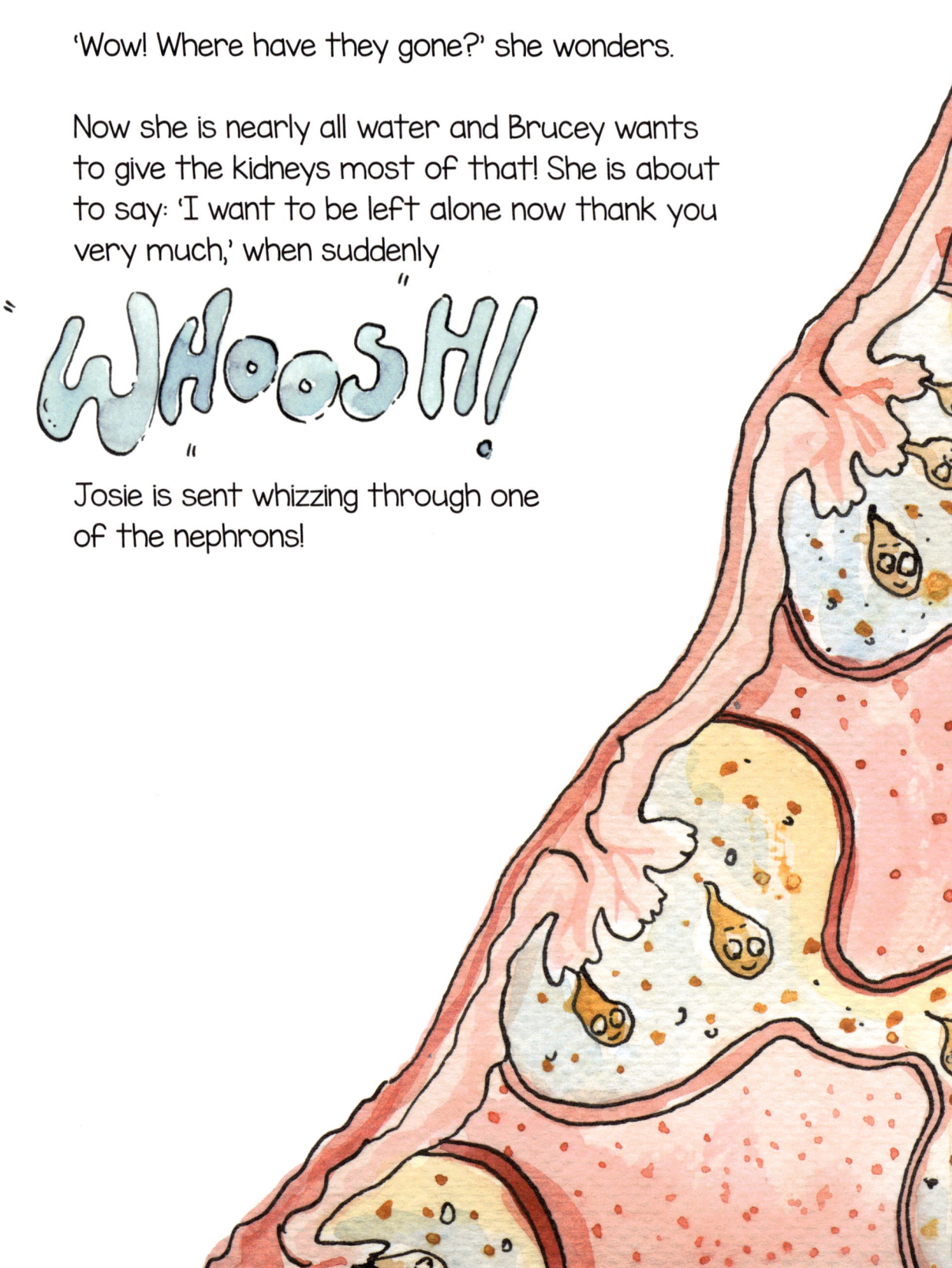

"WHOOSH!"

Josie is sent whizzing through one of the nephrons!

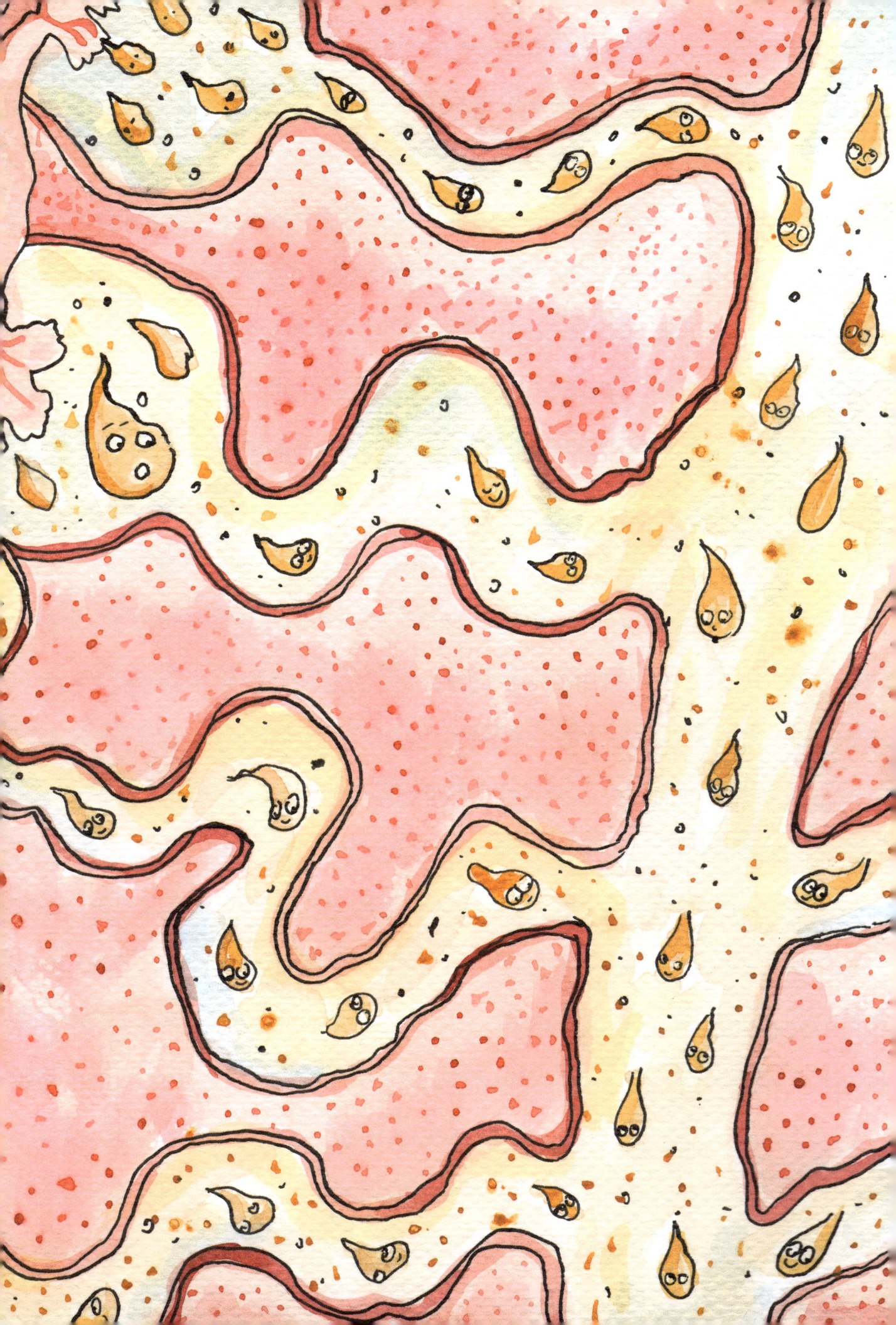

CHAPTER 3

The BIG Hill!

In the meantime... Matthew and his Dad are out in the car picking up his friends. Eventually they arrive at the sledging centre.

More friends are there waiting for Matthew. They all clap and cheer when they see him. This makes him blush. Poor Matthew, he doesn't like a lot of fuss, but all was soon forgotten when he saw the sledges.

They are brightly coloured and have wheels so that they can whizz down the grass hills.

Dad comes along with the staff from the sledging hut. They are all given helmets to wear. They are needed to protect their heads in case they fall off the sledges and bump their heads. Matthew's friend James doesn't want to wear a helmet. 'That's sissy and I don't like the colour,' he says. The instructor takes no notice of him and carries on fitting the children with their helmets.

Soon everyone is ready. 'Come on boys,' calls the instructor, 'climb onto the trailer so we can take you up to the top of the big hill.'

James starts to climb on but the instructor stops him.

'Why can't I get on?' says James in a huff.
'It is great fun to ride a bicycle or a pony, James, but if you fall and bang your head you can do some nasty damage. That is why when people do certain sports, they need to protect their head by wearing a helmet.'

James doesn't want a cracked head. He realises he is being rather silly, so agrees to put on his helmet and doesn't even mind the colour.

An old tractor tows the trailer up the big slope.
It chug, chug, chugs to the top of the hill.

'Look at that!' yells Matthew
when the tractor stops.

They jump off the trailer and stand at the top of an enormous hill. They can see for

MILES

In front of them is a big track in the grass, which looks as though it goes on forever! Who was going to be the first to go?

CHAPTER 4

Josie Juice Explores!

Josie Juice is exploring a nephron in Matthew's kidney! She is being swept along a tiny tube with Brucey Blood.

'What are all these tiny bits doing floating along with me Brucey?'

'They have a very special name: 'Electrolytes.' 'Electrolytes?' says Josie.

'Yes' says Brucey, 'without them Matthew's body wouldn't work properly.'

Sometimes when you have been sick or quite unwell, the electrolytes get muddled up, which can make you feel even worse.

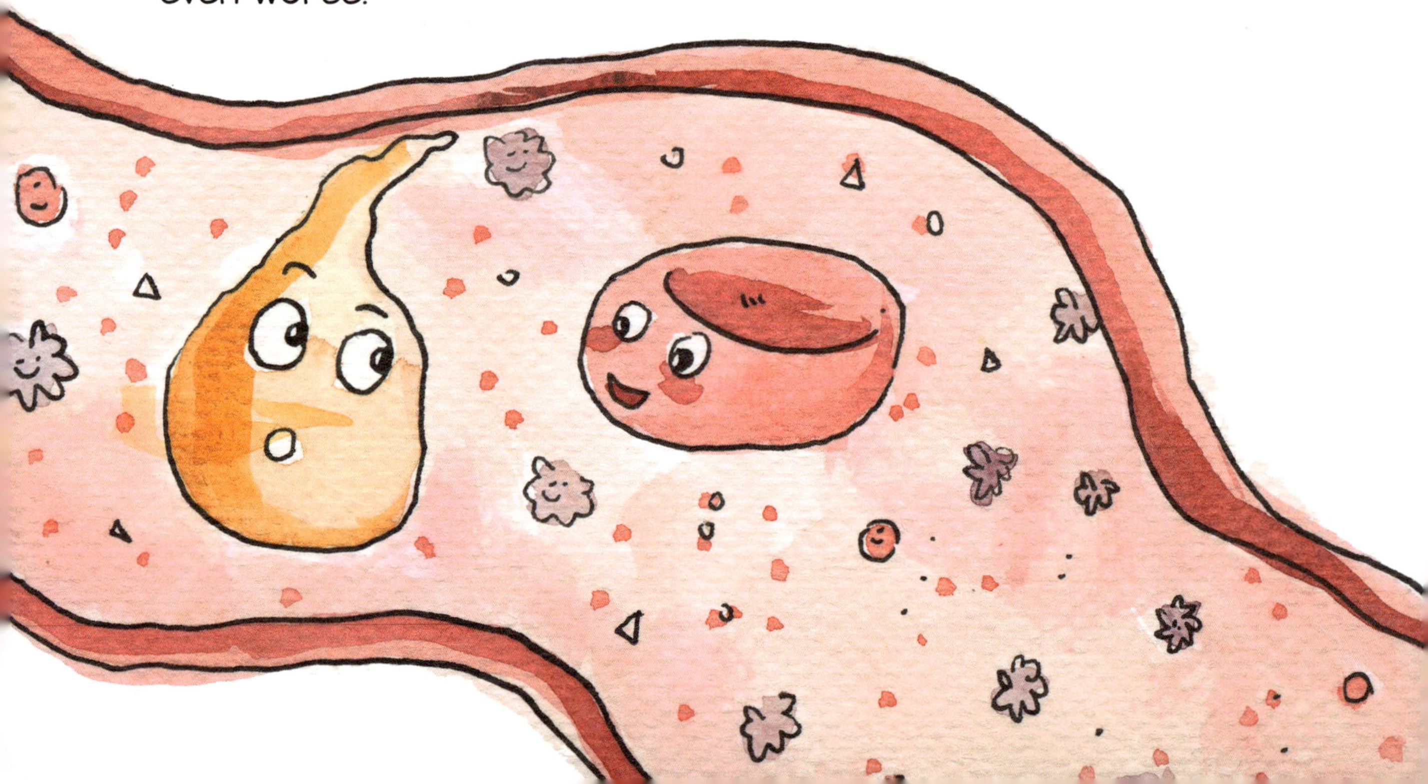

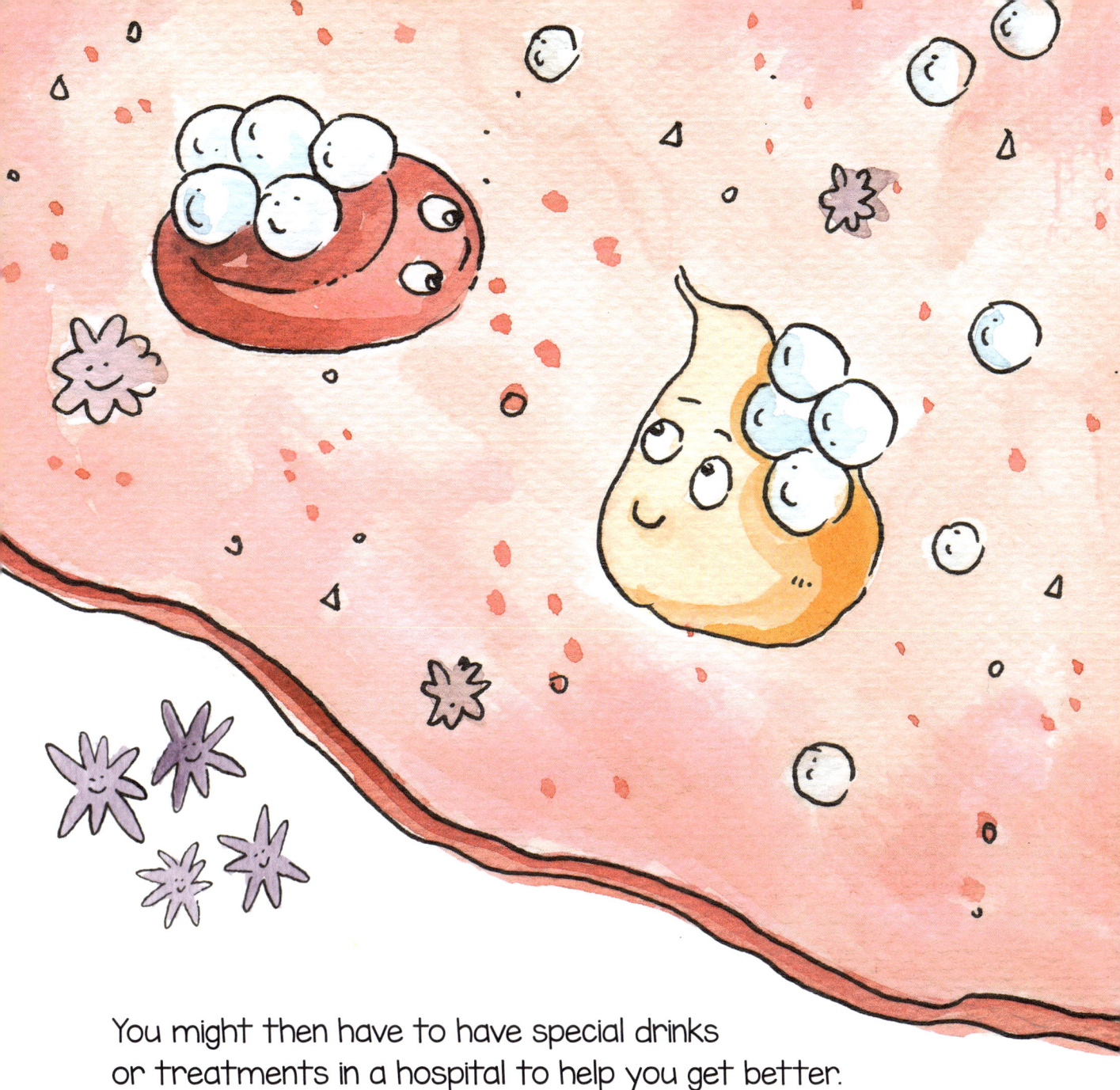

You might then have to have special drinks
or treatments in a hospital to help you get better.

Josie Juice and Brucey Blood are also doing lots of other
important things for Matthew. They are carrying the oxygen
and food needed for the cells that make the muscles in his
arms, legs and heart work properly.

What Josie hasn't realised is that the nephron is slowly sieving
Brucey Blood. It decides what can stay with Brucey and what
needs to be removed from the body as pee. There are LOTS
of complicated things going on inside Matthew's body while he
was enjoying sledging with his friends.

CHAPTER 5

Whizzing Down the Hill!

Matthew and his friends stand at the top of the big hill. They are all a bit nervous to start with; none of them want to be the first to go. In the end Matthew says 'OK, I'll go!'

He sits in a bright red sledge with his helmet well secured. The sledge has special wheels so that it would run easily over all the grassy bumps. There are handles on each side and Matthew grips them tightly.

3! ...2! ...1! ..GO!!

shout his friends together.

The sledge zooms off the bank.

It trundles and bounces along, whizzing down the hill. The world becomes a blur for Matthew. His teeth chatter together, the wind rushes past his face making his eyes water.

He shouts and screams in delight. Holding on to the sledge tightly, he can't believe how much fun this is.

The end is in sight. 'Ahhh,' screeches Matthew, 'will I stop in time?'

He doesn't need to worry for long as the ground levels off and the sledge comes to a stop. His turn is over. His cheeks are bright red and he is filled with excitement.

'That was brill,' he says, and is eager to get back up to the top to do it all again. However, he has to be patient and wait for his friends to have their turn. It isn't long before they are all climbing onto the trailer again. The tractor chug, chug, chugs back up the hill.

Soon it is time for lunch. They are very hungry.
They are also hot, sweaty and in need of a drink.

CHAPTER 6

Toilet and things!

Matthew sits down with his friends for lunch and drinks a large glass of water. 'Oh that's better. I really needed that. This sledging is hard work and makes you sweaty.' His kidneys notice he has swallowed some water. Now they have to decide if his body needs all of it or whether they should get rid of some.

If you kept all the fluids you drank you would start to look like a blobby balloon full of water!

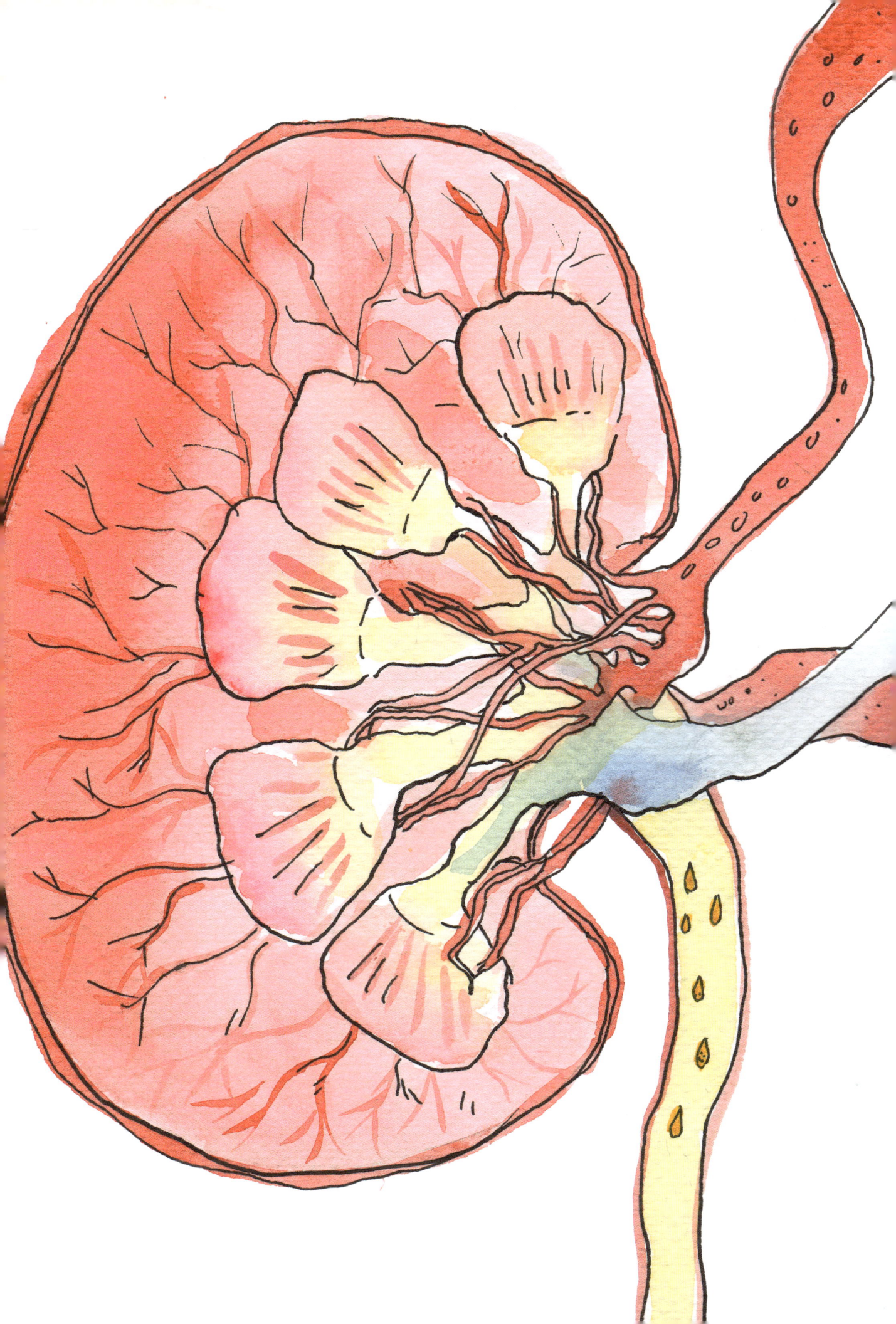

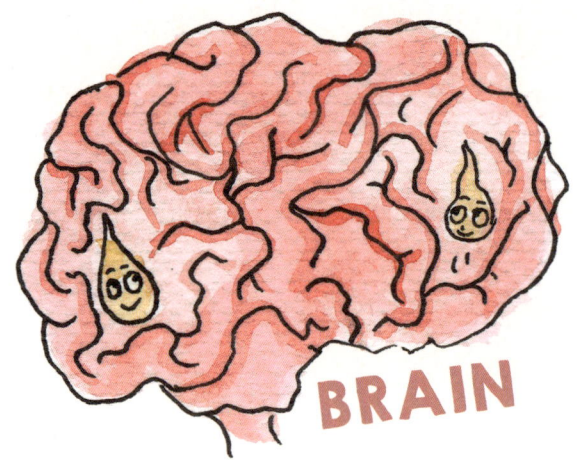

BRAIN

Josie Juice has spent the last few hours visiting different parts of Matthew and only a little bit of her has returned to his kidneys.

The rest of her is scattered all over Matthew's body. When the wind blew in his face as he sledged down the hill, a little drop of Josie had even come out through Matthew's eyes as tears.

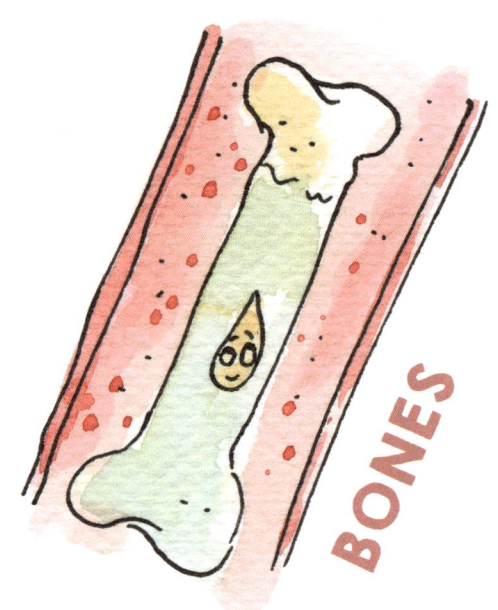

BONES

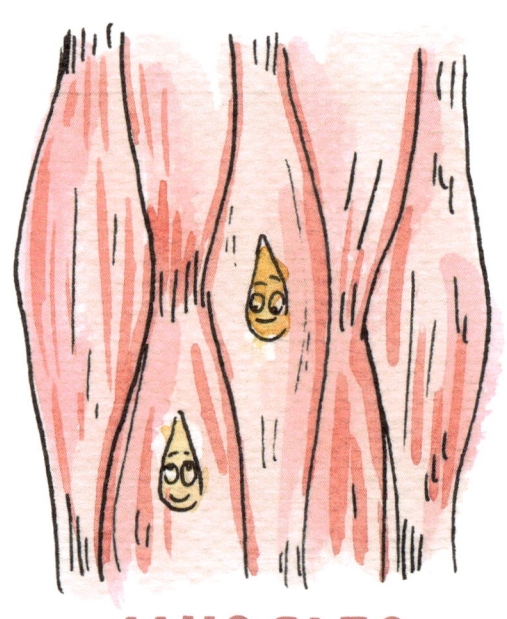

MUSCLES

The kidney decides it is time to get rid of some of the water Matthew has been drinking. It sends it off to some special little tubes called ureters. By this time the water is known as urine, although a lot of us call it pee!
With a

the small bit of Josie slides down the long ureter with the rest of the water. It ends up in a bag called the bladder with a

The bladder collects the pee from the kidney and keeps it there until it is half full. Josie Juice enjoys sploshing around in the bladder but wonders where she might go next? She had left Brucey Blood at the nephron in the kidney and was beginning to feel a little lonely without him.

Matthew's bladder is getting quite full. When there is quite a lot of urine in the bladder special muscles try to squeeze it down another tube called the urethra.

Luckily we have a special tap. This has an interesting name: the external sphincter.

The little tap stops us from wetting our pants while the bladder is collecting urine.

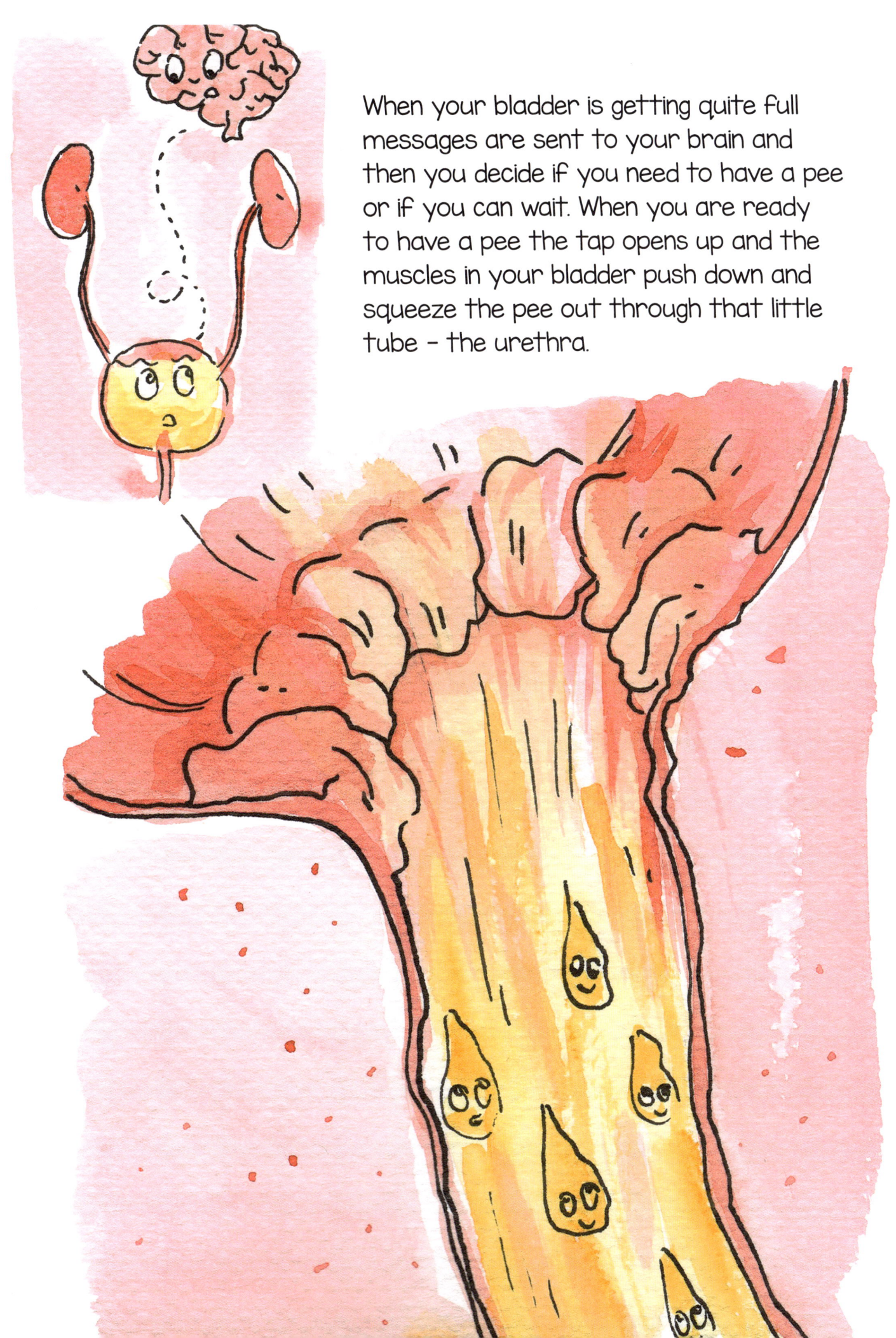

When your bladder is getting quite full messages are sent to your brain and then you decide if you need to have a pee or if you can wait. When you are ready to have a pee the tap opens up and the muscles in your bladder push down and squeeze the pee out through that little tube – the urethra.

The bladder sends messages to Matthew's brain: 'Matthew! You need to have a pee!' However, Matthew is having so much fun he doesn't want to leave his friends to go to the toilet. The messages become stronger and stronger.

MATTHEW

YOU REALLY NEED TO HAVE A PEE!

Matthew tries to ignore the messages. He sits at the table jiggling and wriggling.

He feels a wet patch in his pants. Oh dear...Matthew has done a very tiny pee! He has left it so long to go to the toilet that his bladder got too full and the tap has let a little bit of urine out! Matthew runs to the toilet, and before you can shout

HIPPOPOTAMUS

he has a massive pee! He flushes the toilet and washes his hands. He then has to go and tell his Dad about his damp pants. He starts to cry. Some more of Josie Juice pops out in his tears.

Dad gives him a cuddle.

'Never mind Matthew, it only happened because you are having such good fun,' says his Dad. 'Here's a dry pair, but Matthew, don't wait so long next time!'

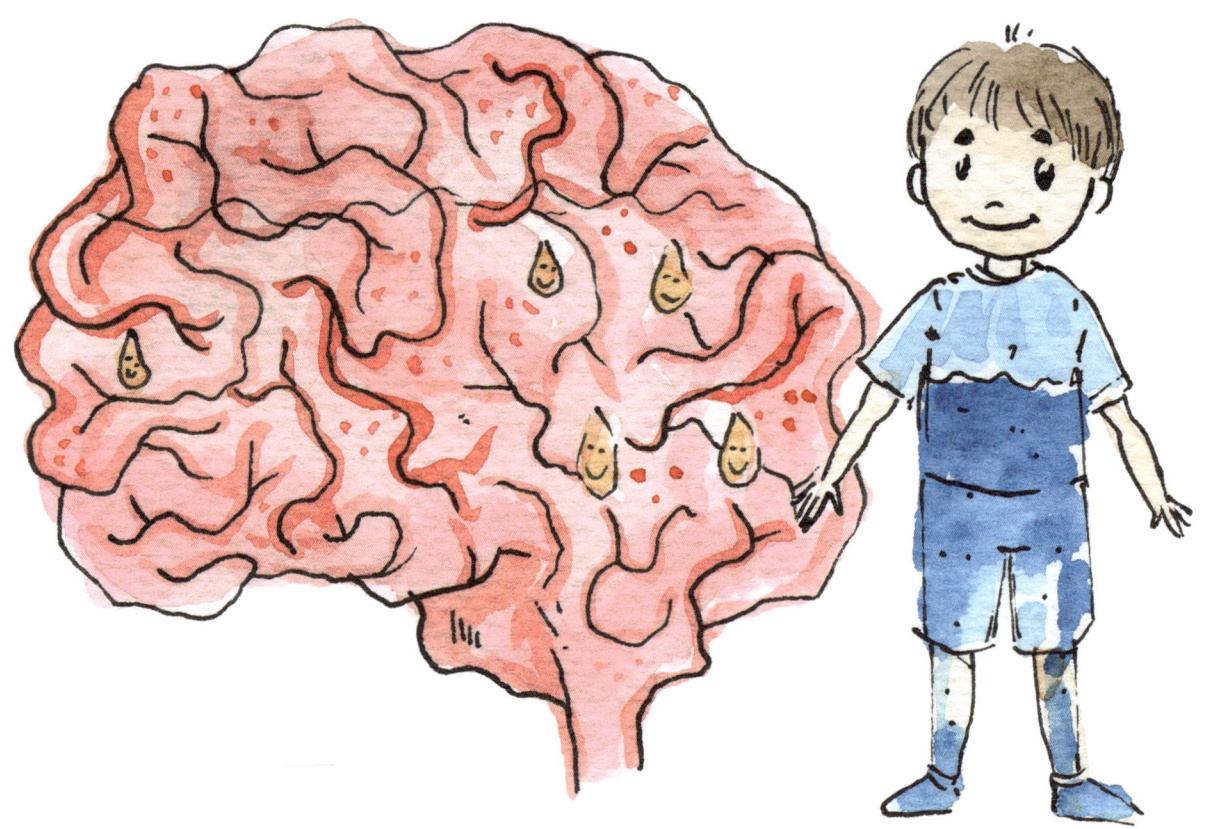

All the boys eat a LARGE lunch and have BIG glasses of water to replace the energy and the fluid they lost running around and sweating during the morning.

'OK lads,' shouts the instructor, 'who is up for some more sledging?'

'WE ARE!' yell the boys. They run out and pile onto the trailer (complete with helmets). Although a tiny bit of Josie is now in the toilet, most of her is still enjoying her time in Matthew's body. I wonder if a bit more of Josie Juice will sneak out through his eyes when he goes down the hill again?

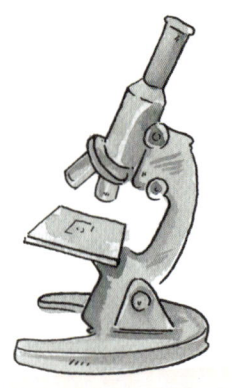

Where does Josie go?

 1/4 litre lost through breathing

 1/2 litre through sweat

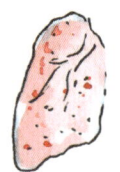 the lungs are about 83% water

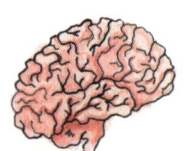 the brain is 73% water

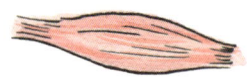 his muscles are 79% water

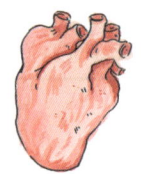 the heart is composed of 73% water

 The skin contains 64% water

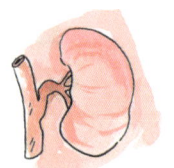 the kidneys are also 79% water

 and even the bones are watery, they are 31% water

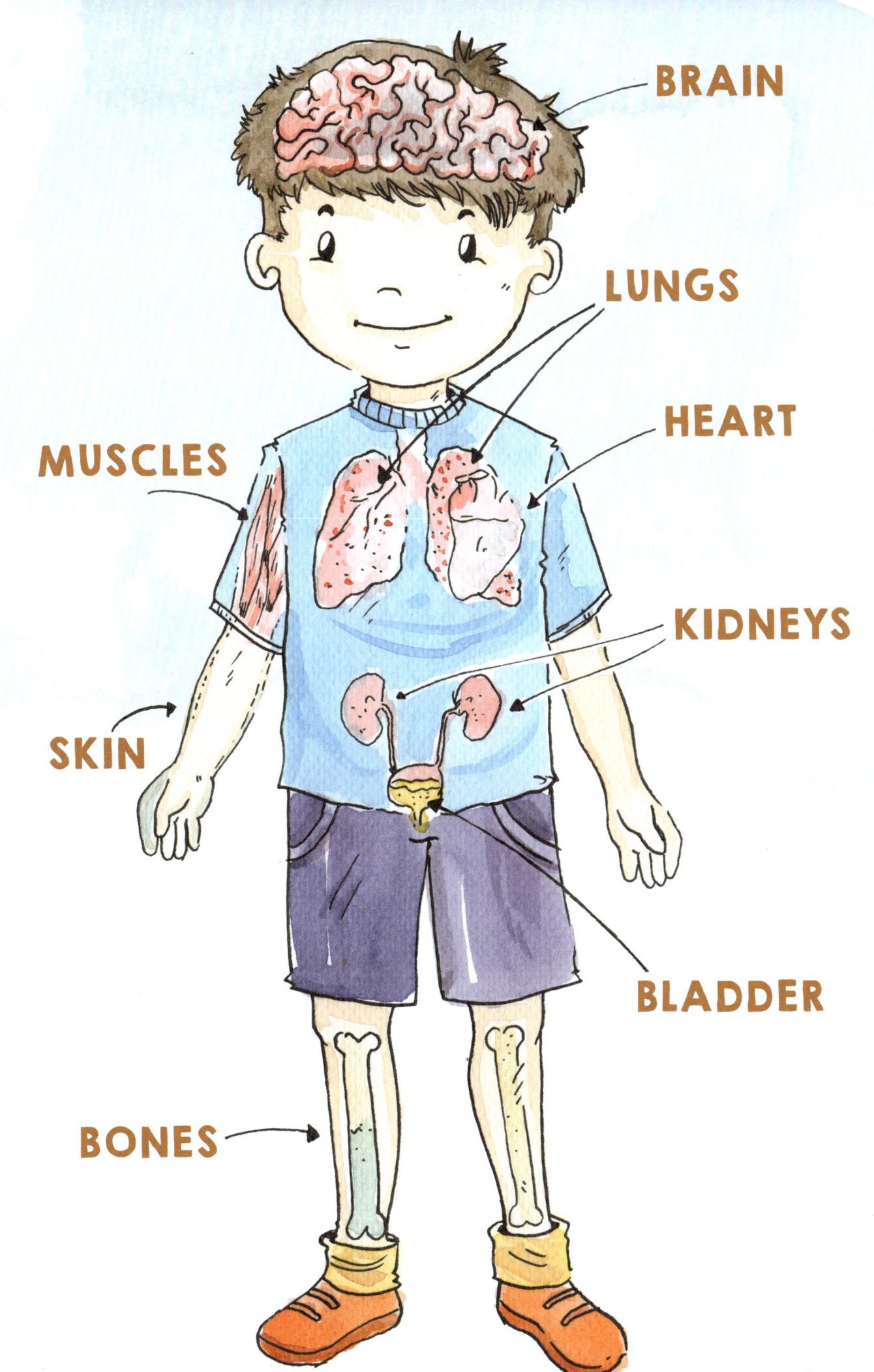

BRAIN

LUNGS

HEART

MUSCLES

KIDNEYS

SKIN

BLADDER

BONES

What does it all mean?

Bladder This is where the urine (pee) is stored until you pass it i.e. into a nappy or toilet for example. In an adult, the bladder might be able to hold 0.5 litres of urine before there is a feeling to pass it.

Blood is the red liquid that flows around the inside of your body and you can see it if you cut yourself. It flows like a river through tiny elastic tubes (known as vessels) around your body pumped along by the heart. It takes things like the air that we breathe and the food that we eat to different parts of the body to help keep us alive. It also plays an important role in protecting us against infection.

Brain this is found inside your head. It controls most of the things your body does like moving your arms and legs; or feel things like if you have pain or something is hot. It controls things like emotion, speech and thought.

Cells these are very tiny. They are the smallest part of a plant or animal, each one containing millions of cells. The human body contains billions of these and are essential to perform the complex tasks necessary for life.

Electrolytes These are tiny and can be found in the blood. They play a very important role in keeping the body healthy. If you become ill and lose a lot of fluid (like vomiting for example), they become unbalanced which can then stop your body working correctly. Sometimes people need medical help to get the electrolytes balanced again.

External Sphincter External means outside. Sphincter is a ring of muscle that can be found around an opening. In the story about the kidneys with Matthew, the ring of muscle is on the outside of the bladder. It stays tight and keeps the urine (pee) in your bladder until you are ready to use the toilet. When it gets the message that you want to use the toilet, it relaxes and lets the urine out...unless of course you are like Matthew and wait tooooo long!

Heart This is found in your chest area. It is made of muscle and pumps the blood around your body...even when you are asleep!

Kidney there are usually 2 of these in a body but you can live perfectly normal with just one. They are bean shaped. Kidney's help keep the blood clean and regulate the body's fluid balance. Anything that isn't needed is passed out of the body as urine. They also produce hormones which are used in the regulation of red blood cell production and blood pressure.

Lungs Your lungs are the two sac like organs inside your chest which fill with air when you breathe in. They supply the body with an important gas known as oxygen and eliminate waste air including carbon dioxide. Plus they play an important role when you are talking.

Microscope these are used to make very small things look bigger so that more detail can be seen.

Minerals These are found in foods. They are an essential part of a diet to maintain a healthy body. There are at least 20 and include calcium, iron, zinc, potassium and sodium. Some are only needed in tiny amounts. A well-balanced diet will provide all that you need.

Muscle There are three types:
1. Skeletal muscle is a piece of tissue inside your body which is connected to your bones by tendons and gives your body shape. You use these muscles to make your body move.
2. Smooth muscles are in the walls of internal organs for example the intestine (peristalsis action which moves the food along); blood vessels; and the bladder.
3. Cardiac muscle which helps keep the heart beating thousands of times a day.

Nephrons these are tiny little tubes found in the kidney. They filter the blood and also decide what can stay in the body and what needs to be sent to the bladder via the kidney. This process produces urine (pee).

Oesophagus is the part of your body that carries the food from the throat to the stomach. It is part of the digestive tract. Powerful actions of the muscles in the wall of the oesophagus propel food and liquids down towards the stomach for digestion.

Oxygen This is a gas and is in the air that we breathe. Animals and plants cannot live without oxygen.

Renal Artery Renal is a word used to describe things related to the kidneys. Arteries are the tubes that carry the blood from your heart to the rest of your body. So the 'renal artery' is the tube that carries the blood from your heart to the kidneys.

Small Intestine the first and longest part of the intestine. It is in 3 parts - the duo-denum, jejunum, and ileum. This is where most of the important things in your food is digested and then taken (by the blood for example) to where it is needed in your body.

Stomach This is a bit like a sack and is between the oesophagus and the small intestine. Food is mixed together here with liquid known as gastric juices (the big yellow pool) and partly digested before it moves into the small intestine.

Ureter the tube along which urine travels from the kidney to the bladder.

Urethra this is the tube that the urine (pee) travels along from the bladder to the outside of the body – when you have a pee.

Urine also known as pee. This is the pale yellow liquid that comes from the kidneys after cleaning the blood. It is kept in the bladder until you are ready to have a pee. Then it travels down the urethra and into a nappy or toilet for example.

Vitamins These are found naturally in a lot of foods and are also added to other things like breakfast cereals. They are really important, as the body will not work properly if it does not get enough vitamins every day.

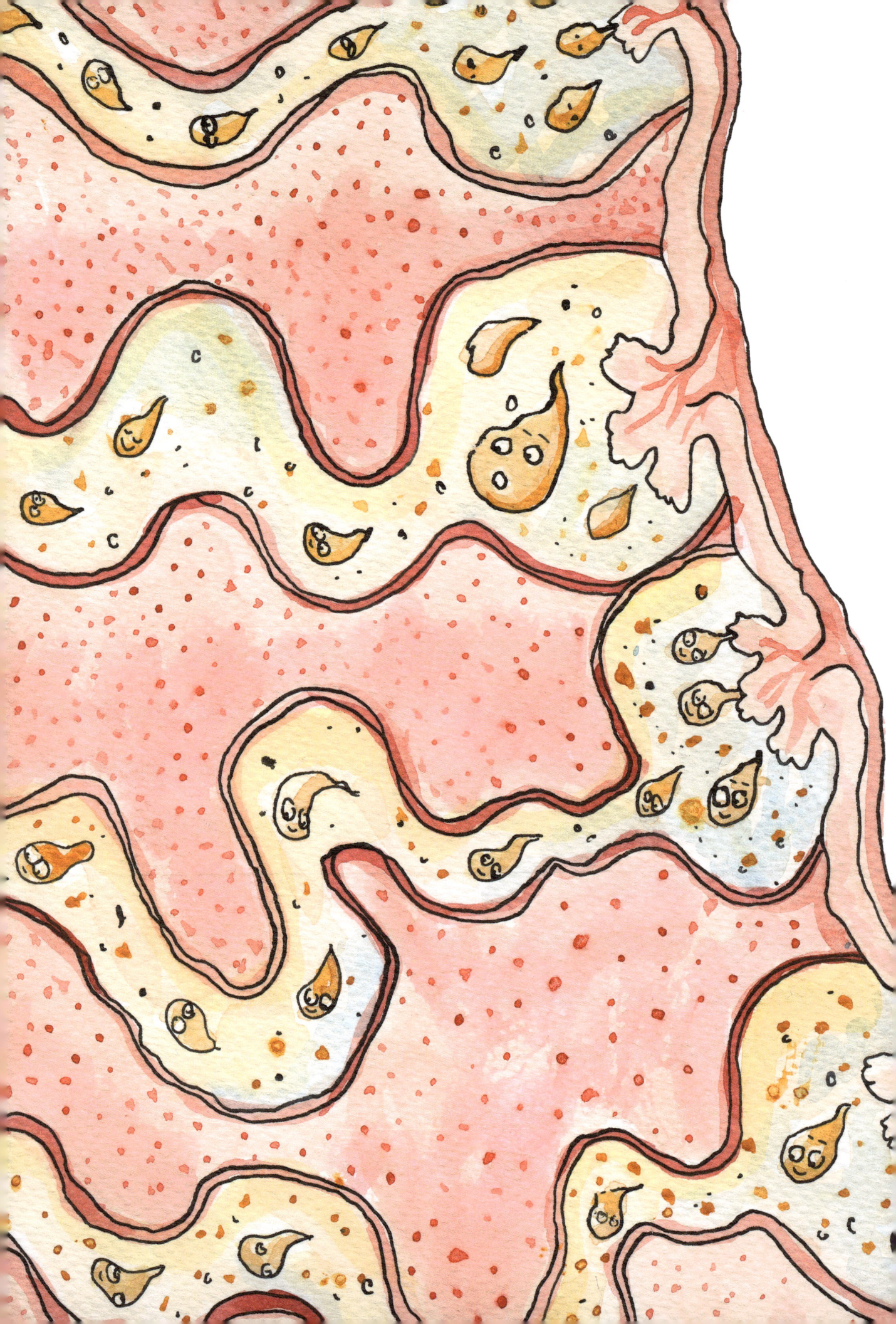

JOSIE JUICE WORDSEARCH

This word search can be photocopied as long as it is for educational purposes and related to the use of the Busy Body Series.

```
E V T P N N E Z K Y H Z O P J
B P A B W I R X E J E E U D C
L Z O Z P A S L G D A N A U K
O E H C B R M G H Q I J D R J
O P N A S B A R H T E R U I T
D S G I J O S Y Y N X O R V K
Q O H L R V R G Q H X J K W U
I D C W V U M C B U Q P T S H
N E G Y X O Z C I L R M P L N
V A E S M X I G I M A E C Q V
N O R H P E N H P N K D T C L
Z Y X C E C L S Y J B V D E U
S E T Y L O R T C E L E K E R
P O X P S M R X I J F X L R R
K F F Q W W C K M L L N Y V F
```

BLADDER
BLOOD
BRAIN
ELECTROLYTES

HEART
KIDNEY
MICROSCOPE
NEPHRON

OXYGEN
URETER
URETHRA
URINE

Other Books by...

The BUSY BODY Series

Suitable for key stage 1 & 2
Written By Heather Hawley
Illustrated by Sarah-Leigh Wills

For more fun & information visit:
www.busybodyseries.co.uk

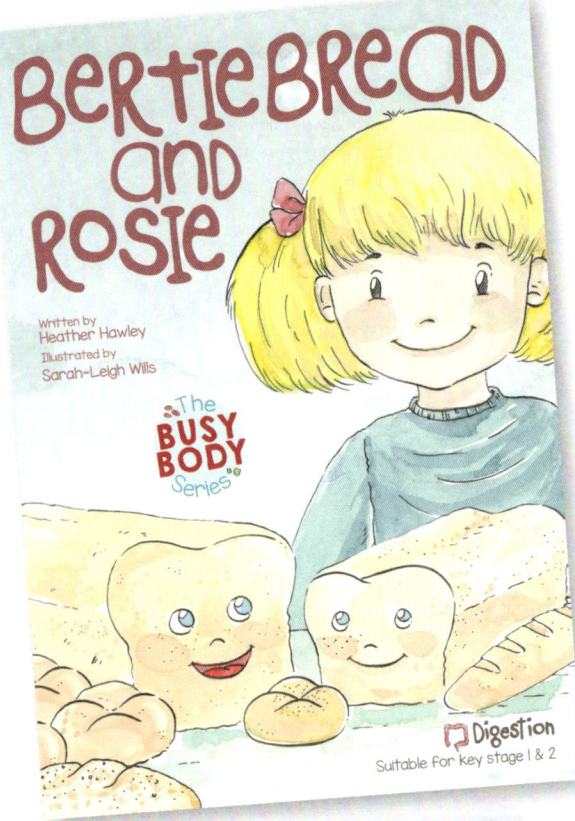

about...

Digestion...

Bertie Breads adventures through Rosie's body are used to explain the process of food from the mouth to the toilet. He meets up with Brucey Blood who explains how bread is used to keep Rosie strong and healthy. The Gas Family and bacteria are used to help illustrate why at times you feel 'windy' during digestion!

ISBN 978-0-9931014-0-3

£6.99

about...

Type I diabetes...

Susie Sugars adventures through Tom's body are used to explain the process of food being turned into glucose (then Susie Glucose!) and how the glucose is used for energy. She meets up with Brucey Blood who explains how insulin is needed to unlock the cells for Susie before she can be used by Tom for energy. Then they find that pancreas cannot produce any insulin and as a result Tom becomes ill. The story continues with Tom going to the surgery then the hospital for diagnosis and treatment of Type I Diabetes and finally back home.

ISBN 978-0-9931014-1-0

£6.99

The Author
Heather...

"I have worked as an Advanced Nurse Practitioner (BSc (Hons) ACNP) in a GP surgery since 1999 and many of the patients I see are children. Working with children in the medical field can be challenging. Sometimes a creative imagination is useful in order to gain their confidence; this can help the children and their parents to understand the condition and the medical interventions we are making. With this in mind I decided to write the Busy Body Series."

The illustrator
Sarah...

"My style of illustration has regularly been referred to as fun and inventive, the 'quirky designer' being a nickname I have regularly heard. My focus is now on childrens books, 98% of my work these days is just that, and I couldnt think of anything better, a complete excuse for me NOT to let my mind grow up!! I love creating educational books for children, in fact its now a passion of mine, helping them understand through my illustrations. ... and I LOVE music & Haribo!"

Find out more at: www.busybodyseries.co.uk